Finance for Non-Financial Managers In A Week

Roger Mason

The Teach Yo　　　　 ....es has been trusted around the world for over 60 years. This series of 'In A Week' business books is designed to help people at all levels and around the world to further their careers. Learn in a week, what the experts learn in a lifetime.

Roger Mason is a Chartered Certified Accountant and has many years' practical experience as a Financial Director. He now lectures on financial and business topics. In addition, he has edited a financial publication and written many books.

Finance for Non-Financial Managers

Roger Mason

www.inaweek.co.uk

Hodder Education

338 Euston Road, London NW1 3BH.

Hodder Education is an Hachette UK company

First published in UK 1993 by Hodder Education

First published in US in 2012 by McGraw-Hill Companies, Inc

This edition published 2012.

Previous editions of this book were published by Hodder in 1993, 1998, 2003.

Database right Hodder Education (makers)

The *Teach Yourself* name is a registered trademark of Hachette UK.

British Library Cataloguing in Publication Data: a catalogue record for this title is available from the British Library.

Library of Congress Catalog Card Number: on file.

The publisher has used its best endeavours to ensure that any website addresses referred to in this book are correct and active at the time of going to press. However, the publisher and the author have no responsibility for the websites and can make no guarantee that a site will remain live or that the content will remain relevant, decent or appropriate.

The publisher has made every effort to mark as such all words which it believes to be trademarks. The publisher should also like to make it clear that the presence of a word in the book, whether marked or unmarked, in no way affects its legal status as a trademark.

Every reasonable effort has been made by the publisher to trace the copyright holders of material in this book. Any errors or omissions should be notified in writing to the publisher, who will endeavour to rectify the situation for any reprints and future editions.

Hachette UK's policy is to use papers that are natural, renewable and recyclable products and made from wood grown in sustainable forests. The logging and manufacturing processes are expected to conform to the environmental regulations of the country of origin.

www.hoddereducation.co.uk

Typeset by Cenveo Publisher Services.

Printed in Great Britain by CPI Group (UK) Ltd, Croydon, CR0 4YY

Also available in ebook

Contents

Introduction   2

Sunday   4
An introduction to Profit Statements

Monday   22
An introduction to Balance Sheets

Tuesday   36
Understanding published accounts

Wednesday   50
Accounting ratios and investment decisions

Thursday   68
Cash and the management of working capital

Friday   84
Costing

Saturday   100
Budgets

Surviving in tough times   116
Answers   120
Glossary   121

Introduction

Depending on how far you are willing to stretch the definition, there are well over a million non-financial managers in the UK, with considerably more in other countries. Many of them would like to know more about finance, and the knowledge would help them do their jobs and progress in their careers. There are, of course, a number of books for non-financial managers, but I firmly believe that there is a call for this one, too. I give my own point of view in some areas and I hope that this will be useful and thought-provoking. I am an experienced manager, as well as a speaker and writer on the topics covered, and I hope that this is apparent.

I have a very practical reason for believing that there is a great interest in the subject of this book. Some years ago I wrote a different book for non-financial managers and it was issued in a series with nine other titles on different subjects. I forecast to the publisher that my book would outsell the others. She thought not, but I was proved correct. This makes me sound arrogant but the reason was not the quality of my writing, although I was pleased with the book. Rather it was the demand for the book's title.

A basic understanding of finance is very relevant to our personal lives. It is also important to virtually all managers and supervisors, both junior and senior. This has always been so and its significance has considerably increased in recent years.

Full budgeting by schools and the PFI initiative are examples of its increasing importance in the public sector, and in both public and private sectors it is necessary for managers to be familiar with financial terms. It is essential that managers understand the financial consequences of the decisions that they make. The present tough economic climate means that this has never been more important.

All levels of management are regularly confronted with such queries as:

- Is it in the budget?
- Do we have the resources?
- What is the return on investment?
- What do these figures really mean?
- What are the cash implications?

Some managers have been financially trained but many more wish to increase their level of understanding. Doing so will enable them to become more effective and improve their scope for development and promotion.

This book is written for managers wishing to achieve this. By setting aside a little time each day for a week you should increase your understanding of the basics of finance.

Please note that your learning on Tuesday and Wednesday will be more effective if you have to hand a company's Annual Report and Accounts. It would be helpful if this could be obtained in advance.

The book contains 70 end-of-chapter questions, each with four possible answers. The correct answers are given at the end of the book. I do hope that you attempt them. If you get 60 correct, that is a good score – anything higher is exceptional.

I have enjoyed writing this book and I hope that you enjoy reading it, or at the very least find it useful. My best wishes for your future success.

Roger Mason

SUNDAY

An introduction to Profit Statements

Nearly all private sector businesses are conducted in the hope of making a profit, though of course not all succeed in doing so. Profits and losses, which perhaps should be called surpluses and deficits, are also important to large parts of the public sector and to such bodies as charities and membership organizations. There is of course much more to it, but many managers would say that the point of bookkeeping and accounting is to find out the amount of the profit or loss.

Profit Statements are important and an introduction to them is a very good way of starting the week. The more advanced published accounts will be studied on Tuesday, but today we will study an internal document produced for the managers.

We will work through the following:

- a simple example
- a trading company
- a manufacturing company
- some further concepts explained
- preparing a full example.

A simple example

The heading 'Profit Statement' may be optimistic because it implies that a profit has been made. In some cases it would be more appropriate to call it a Loss Statement.

Profit Statement is the name often given to an internal document setting out the trading activity and results. It is sometimes called the Profit and Loss Account or Income Statement and these are the titles used in the more formal published accounts.

Understanding the principles of a Profit Statement is the first step towards using it to improve future performance. This is covered later in the week but as a first step we will consider a simple example.

Julia Brown writes a book. Her agreement does not provide for royalties, just a fee of £5,000 payable on delivery of the manuscript to the publisher. The costs of the enterprise are small and she pays them in cash as she goes. After receipt of the £5,000 her Profit Statement may well look like the following:

	£	£
Income		5,000
Less costs:		
Typing costs	600	
Stationery	100	
Travel	200	
Postage	30	
Telephone	40	
Miscellaneous	120	
		1,090
Net Profit before Tax		3,910

The profit (or loss) is the difference between money received and all the money paid out. Julia Brown may need the Profit Statement for her bank and for Her Majesty's Revenue and Customs (HMRC). She may use the information herself. For example, if she has spent 391 hours working on the book her time has been rewarded at the rate of £10 per hour.

A trading company

Numerous very small businesses do prepare simple Profit Statements in the manner of the previous example. However, there is another step when things are bought and sold.

It is essential that the costs shown in the Profit Statement relate only to goods sold during the period. All Profit Statements cover a defined period with a specified starting date and a specified closing date. For published accounts this period is often a year but for internal documents it can be whatever period is considered most useful.

Many businesses produce quarterly Profit Statements, but it may be desirable to produce them monthly or even weekly. Some intensively managed retailers, such as Tesco and Asda, produce key profit information on a daily basis. They withdraw items and change displays according to the results shown.

A distorted result will be given if costs include articles purchased (and paid for) but still in stock at the end of the period. This is overcome by counting stock at the beginning and end of the period. The cost of sales is calculated by adding purchases to the opening stock, then subtracting the closing stock.

If there has been any theft or other form of stock shrinkage, the cost of sales will be increased accordingly.

Sometimes the calculation as far as Gross Profit is shown in a separate Trading Account. However, the following simple example shows everything in one Profit Statement.

A Borough Council Leisure Centre operates a bar and prepares monthly Profit Statements. Sales in the month of July were £30,000 and purchases in the same month were £20,000.

Stock of food and drink at 30 June was £10,000 and at 31 July it was £9,000. Wages were £4,000, insurance was £1,500, and the total of all other overheads was £3,000.

The Profit Statement for July was as follows:

	£	£
Sales		30,000
Stock at 30 June	10,000	
Purchases	20,000	
	30,000	
Less stock at 31 July	9,000	
		21,000
Gross Profit		9,000
Less Overheads:		
Wages	4,000	
Insurance	1,500	
All other	3,000	
		8,500
Net Profit		500

A manufacturing company

It is only a small step to set out the Profit Statement of a manufacturing company. It is essential that the cost of manufacturing must exactly relate to the goods sold. The cost of these goods, no more and no less, must be brought into the Profit Statement.

Probably, stocktakes will be necessary at the beginning and end of the period. However, according to circumstances, this may not be necessary. If internal controls are good a calculated stock figure may sometimes be used, though the results are never quite so accurate or dependable. It is most likely to be done when the results are produced very quickly.

The following example shows the principles. Sometimes the manufacturing costs are shown in a separate Manufacturing Account but in this straightforward example they are included in the Profit Statement.

Chiltern Manufacturing Company Ltd manufactures and sells household goods. Sales in the year to 31 December 2011 were £750,000. Purchases of raw materials and components in the year were £300,000. Stock at 31 December 2010 was £280,000 and at 31 December 2011 it was £320,000.

Wages of production staff were £200,000, power costs were £60,000 and other production costs were £80,000. Salaries of salesmen, administration staff and management totalled £70,000 and other overheads totalled £85,000.

The Profit Statement for the year to 31 December 2011 is as follows:

	£	£
Sales		750,000
Stock at 31.12.10	280,000	
Purchases	300,000	
	580,000	
Less stock at 31.12.11	320,000	
	260,000	
Production wages	200,000	
Power costs	60,000	
Other production costs	80,000	
Cost of Manufacturing		600,000
		150,000
Less Overheads:		
Salaries	70,000	
Other overheads	85,000	
		155,000
Net Loss before Tax		(5,000)

(Note that the brackets indicate a minus figure.)

Key points so far

- There are definite starting and finishing dates.
- Total Sales appears at the top.
- Profit or Loss appears at the bottom.
- Only expenditure on goods actually sold is included.

Some further concepts explained

All the examples so far have been extremely simple but unfortunately real life is often more complicated. It is necessary to be familiar with certain further principles that are likely to be incorporated into many Profit Statements.

Accruals (costs not yet entered)

Examples so far have assumed that all costs are paid out as they are incurred, but this is unrealistic. Invoices are submitted after the event and some will not have been entered into the books when they are closed off.

This problem is overcome by adding in an allowance for these costs. The uninvoiced costs are called accruals.

Let us take as an example a company whose electricity bill is around £18,000 per quarter. Let us further assume that accounts are made up to 31 December and that the last electricity bill was up to 30 November. The accountant will accrue £6,000 for electricity used but not billed.

If electricity invoices in the period total £60,000 the added £6,000 will result in £66,000 being shown in the Profit Statement.

Prepayments (costs entered in advance)

A prepayment is the exact opposite of an accrual. Costs may have been entered into the books for items where the benefit has not yet been received. An example is an invoice for production materials delivered after stocktaking.

Consider an insurance premium of £12,000 paid on 1 December for 12 months' cover in advance. If the Profit Statement is made up to 31 December the costs will have been overstated by $\frac{11}{12}$ x £12,000 = £11,000. The accountant will reduce the costs accordingly. These reductions are called prepayments.

Bad debt reserves and sales ledger reserves

Many businesses sell on credit, and at the end of the period of the Profit Statement money will be owed by customers. Unfortunately not all of this money will necessarily be received. Among the possible reasons are:

- bad debts
- an agreement that customers may deduct a settlement discount if payment is made by a certain date

- the customers may claim that there were shortages, or that they received faulty goods; perhaps goods were supplied on a sale-or-return basis.

The prudent accountant will make reserves to cover these eventualities, either a bad debt reserve or sales ledger reserve. Sales (and profit) will be reduced by an appropriate amount.

Time will tell whether the reserves have been fixed at a level that was too high, too low, or just right. If the reserves were too cautious there will be an extra profit to bring into a later Profit Statement. If the reserves were not cautious enough there will be a further cost (and loss) to bring into a later Profit Statement.

Depreciation

Fixed assets are those that will have a useful and productive life longer than the period of the Profit Statement. Examples are factory machinery, computers, motor vehicles and so on.

It would obviously be wrong to charge all the costs of fixed assets to the Profit Statement in the year of purchase. The problem is overcome by charging only a proportion in each year of the expected useful life of the asset.

There are different methods of doing this calculation but the simplest, and most common, is the straight-line method. For example, let us consider an item of equipment costing

£300,000 with an expected useful life of five years. The Profit Statement for each year would be charged with £60,000.

This is one of many examples of how profit accounting may differ from the equivalent position in cash. It is quite possible to be profitable and still run out of cash. This will be examined later in the week.

Prudence and the matching of costs to income

Earlier it was explained that costs must be fairly matched to sales. This is so that the costs of the goods actually sold, and only those costs, are brought into the Profit Statement. This is very important, and sometimes very difficult to achieve.

Consider a major building project lasting four years and for which the contractor will be paid £60,000,000. Costs over the four years are expected to be £55,000,000 and the anticipated profit is £5,000,000. Almost certainly the contractor will receive various stage payments over the four years.

This poses a multitude of accounting problems and there is more than one accounting treatment. The aim must be to bring in both revenue and costs strictly as they are earned and incurred. Accounting standards provide firm rules for the published accounts.

The full £60,000,000 will not be credited until the work is complete. In fact there will probably be a retention and it will be necessary to make a reserve for retention work. The final cost and profit may not be known for some years.

Conventions of prudent accounting should ensure that profits are only recognized when they have clearly been earned. Losses on the other hand should be recognized as soon as they can be realistically foreseen. Failure to act on this convention has led to scandals and nasty surprises for investors, the collapse of Enron being just one example.

Before leaving this section, tick off the following boxes to confirm that you understand the principles.

- Accruals are costs incurred, but not yet in the books. ❑
- Prepayments are costs in the books, but not yet incurred. ❑
- Profit is reduced by expected bad debts. ❑

- Depreciation is a book entry to reduce the value of fixed assets. □
- Profit accounting may differ from cash accounting. □
- Profit Statements should be prudent. □
- Costs must be matched to income. □

Preparing a full example

Sunday is concluded with a slightly more advanced example incorporating the points covered so far.

J. T. Perkins and Son Ltd manufactures and sells pottery. Sales in the year to 31 December 2011 were £800,000. At 31 December 2011 the company expects to issue a credit note for £10,000 for faulty goods that have been delivered. It also believes that £30,000 owing to it will turn out to be a total bad debt. No such expectations existed at 31 December 2010.

Invoices received for parts and raw materials delivered during the year totalled £240,000, but a £20,000 invoice is awaited for a delivery received on 22 December.

Stock at 31 December 2010 was £308,000. Stock at 31 December 2011 was £302,000.

Manufacturing wages were £150,000 and other manufacturing costs were £60,000. Plant and machinery used for manufacturing originally cost £900,000 and is being depreciated at the rate of 10% per year.

Overheads paid have been

Salaries	*£80,000*
Rent	*£70,000*
Insurance	*£60,000*
Other	*£50,000*

Insurance includes a premium of £7,000 for a year in advance paid on 31 December 2011.

J. T. Perkins and Son Ltd

Profit Statement for the year to 31 December 2011

	£	£
Sales		790,000
Stock at 31.12.10	308,000	
Add purchases	260,000	
	568,000	
Less stock at 31.12.11	302,000	
	266,000	
Wages	150,000	
Depreciation of plant and machinery	90,000	
Other manufacturing costs	60,000	
Cost of Sales		566,000
Gross Profit		224,000
Less Overheads:		
Salaries	80,000	
Rent	70,000	
Insurance	53,000	
Other	50,000	
Reserve for bad debts	30,000	
		283,000
Net Loss before Tax		(59,000)

Summary

This Sunday we have been introduced to the basic principles of the following:

- Simple Profit Statements
- Trading companies
- Manufacturing companies
- Accruals and prepayments
- Bad debt reserves and sales ledger reserves
- Depreciation
- Prudence and the matching of costs to income
- An example illustrating most of the principles

Tomorrow, we will take a look at Balance Sheets.

SUNDAY

MONDAY

TUESDAY

WEDNESDAY

THURSDAY

FRIDAY

SATURDAY

Fact-check (answers at the back)

1. To what is the term 'Profit Statement' given?
   a) A published Profit and Loss Account ❏
   b) An internal document setting out the trading activity and results ❏
   c) A statement for the tax authorities ❏
   d) A statement for the shareholders ❏

2. In a Profit Statement, where is the figure for income usually placed?
   a) At the top ❏
   b) At the bottom ❏
   c) On the left ❏
   d) On the right ❏

3. In a Profit Statement of a trading company, to what must the figure for Cost of Sales relate?
   a) Goods stored in the period ❏
   b) Goods purchased in the period ❏
   c) Goods paid for in the period ❏
   d) Goods sold in the period ❏

4. If goods for sale are stolen, how will the Cost of Sales in the Profit Statement be affected?
   a) It will increase ❏
   b) It will decrease ❏
   c) It will not be affected ❏
   d) It will be estimated ❏

5. Which stock figures appear in the Profit Statement of a manufacturing company?
   a) None ❏
   b) Figures for the beginning and end of the period ❏
   c) The figure for the beginning of the period ❏
   d) The figure for the end of the period ❏

6. The telephone bill is usually about £3,000 per quarter. The last invoice received was for the quarter to 31 May. What should be the accrual for the three months to 30 June?
   a) £3,000 ❏
   b) Nothing ❏
   c) £1,000 ❏
   d) £2,000 ❏

7. On 29 December rent of £6,000 was paid in advance for the quarter to the following 31 March. What should be the prepayment for the three months to 31 December?
   a) Nothing ❏
   b) £6,000 ❏
   c) £1,000 ❏
   d) £3,000 ❏

8. The Profit Statement for the month of December included a bad debt reserve of £10,000 in respect of money owed by Smith Ltd. On 17 January Smith Ltd paid in full. What is the effect on the Profit Statement for January?

a) There is no effect ❏
b) A contribution to profit of £5,000 ❏
c) A contribution to profit of £20,000 ❏
d) A contribution to profit of £10,000 ❏

9. A company buys a car for £40,000 and using the straight-line method depreciates it over four years. What is the depreciation charge in the Profit Statement in the second year?

a) £40,000 ❏
b) Nothing ❏
c) £10,000 ❏
d) The square root of £40,000 ❏

10. Which of the following should be reflected in a Profit Statement?

a) Prudence
b) Optimism
c) Pessimism
d) Happiness

SUNDAY

MONDAY

TUESDAY

WEDNESDAY

THURSDAY

FRIDAY

SATURDAY

MONDAY

An introduction to Balance Sheets

The main constituents of a set of accounts are the Profit and Loss Account and the Balance Sheet, which in the published accounts may be called the Statement of Financial Position. The Balance Sheet is extremely important and fulfils a completely different function from the Profit Statement. If someone wants answers to questions such as 'What are the assets?' or 'Is the Company safe?' it is a very good place to start.

A Balance Sheet gives details of the assets and liabilities of the business, and this detailed information is often very valuable to the users of accounts. It also reveals the 'net worth' of the business, though perhaps it would be more accurate to say that it does so according to sometimes controversial accounting rules. When a business is sold it is rare for the sum realized to be the same as the 'net worth' according to the Balance Sheet.

Today we will study the Balance Sheet and cover the following:

- what is a Balance Sheet?
- two accounting rules explained
- a simple example
- some further concepts explained
- test your knowledge of Balance Sheets.

What is a Balance Sheet?

The clue is in the name. A Balance Sheet is a listing of all the balances in the accounting system, and what is more it must balance. The debit balances must equal the credit balances, or put another way the assets must equal the liabilities. If they do not, a mistake has been made.

A freeze-frame picture

Unlike the Profit Statement, the Balance Sheet does not cover a trading period. It is a snapshot of the financial position at a precise moment and the date is always given as part of the heading. It is usually produced to coincide with the last day of the trading period.

To complete the photographic analogy, the Balance Sheet is like a freeze-frame picture of the finances of an enterprise. If the picture were to be taken a day earlier or a day later, different financial details would be revealed.

Format of the Balance Sheet

A long time ago it was the custom to set out the figures side by side. The assets (debit balances) went on the right-hand side and the liabilities (credit balances) went on the left-hand side. The two columns of course added up to the same figure.

You will not see a Balance Sheet displayed in this way because Balance Sheets are now shown in a vertical format. The whole thing adds down to the net worth of the business, which is shown at the bottom. There are still two figures which must be the same and which prove that the Balance Sheet balances.

Grouping of figures

Of course not every individual balance is listed in the Balance Sheet. If they were, the Balance Sheet of Marks and Spencer PLC would cover hundreds of pages. For example, a company may have six different bank accounts, all overdrawn by £100,000. The total of all these overdrafts would be shown as just one figure of £600,000.

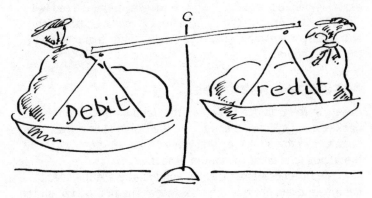

Two accounting rules explained

In order to improve your understanding of Balance Sheets you must be familiar with the following two fundamental accounting rules.

- For every debit there must be a credit.
- Balance Sheet assets are debit balances and Balance Sheet liabilities are credit balances.

Debit and credit balances

If a moment of levity could be excused, the first rule of double-entry bookkeeping is said to be that debit is nearest the window and credit is nearest the door and I was certainly told this on my first morning as a trainee. It is of course only true if you sit with your left shoulder nearest the glass and in any case computers have probably made the joke obsolete. The real first rule of double-entry bookkeeping is that for every debit there must be a credit. Accountancy students are traditionally told this on their very first day. This means that an accounting entry always involves one account being debited and another account being credited. Scientists sometimes help themselves to remember this by thinking of the law of physics: 'every action has an equal and opposite reaction'.

For example, let us consider what happens when a £20,000 car is purchased. The Motor Vehicles account (which is an asset) is debited with £20,000. The bank account is credited with £20,000. At this stage you might be confused by which entries are debits and which are credits. This is explained in the next section.

Assets and liabilities

Assets in the Balance Sheet are the debit balances in the bookkeeping system. Liabilities in the Balance Sheet are credit balances in the bookkeeping system. This is probably exactly the opposite of what you would expect.

In the Profit Statement, sales and income are the credit balances: costs are the debit balances. The net total of all the balances is the profit or loss.

This one figure goes into the Balance Sheet as a single item. A profit is a credit which is listed with the liabilities. This too is probably exactly the opposite of what you would expect.

The explanation is that the profit belongs to someone outside the business. If the Balance Sheet is for a company, the profit belongs to the shareholders. It may one day be paid to them in the form of a dividend or by return of capital on the winding up of the company.

A simple example

John Brown commences business as a gardener on 1 July 2012, using the name Cotswold Gardeners. On his first day he pays £6,000 capital into the business. He buys a motor van for £5,000 and a motor mower for £500. They are immediately second-hand so he depreciates them by 20%.

By the end of the gardening season on 31 October he has invoiced his customers £7,000 and been paid in full. His costs have been £2,000, of which he has paid £1,700 and still owes £300.

During the four months he has taken £4,000 out of the business for his living expenses.

Look at the following Balance Sheet and, with a pencil, make sure that you understand how each of the figures is calculated. The figure for profit is after deducting £1,100 depreciation. You should particularly notice that:

● The Balance Sheet is headed and dated, and it balances.
● The creditor of £300 is money owing by the business. It is an accrual, which is one of the things that we studied yesterday.

- The business is separate from John Brown's personal affairs. This is why the payment of £4,000 living expenses to John Brown takes money out of the business and affects the Balance Sheet.

John Brown Trading as Cotswold Gardeners
Balance Sheet at 31 October 2012

	£	£
Fixed Assets		
Motor vehicle	4,000	
Motor mower	400	
		4,400
Current Assets		
Bank account	1,800	
Less Current Liabilities		
Creditor	300	
		1,500
		5,900
Capital employed		
Capital paid in at 1/7/12	6,000	
Add profit since 1/7/12	3,900	
	9,900	
Less drawings since 1/7/12	4,000	
		5,900

Some further concepts explained

Balance Sheets that will be audited and published are laid out according to certain rules and we will look at these tomorrow. Today, we are concerned with Balance Sheets prepared just for management use. It will be very helpful if you are completely familiar with the following concepts.

Fixed assets and depreciation

Fixed assets are grouped together in the Balance Sheet and one total is given for the net value of all of them. Examples of fixed assets are:

- freehold property
- plant and machinery
- computers
- motor vehicles.

They are assets that will have a value to the business over a long period, usually understood to be any time longer than a year.

They do usually lose their value, either with the passage of time (e.g. a lease), with use (e.g. a piece of machinery that wears out) or due to obsolescence (e.g. computers). Therefore, as we saw yesterday, they are written off over a number of years. Depreciation is a book entry and no cash is involved. The entry is:

- debit depreciation (thus reducing profit)
- credit the asset (thus reducing the value of the asset).

Current assets

Different types of current asset are listed separately in the Balance Sheet with one total being shown for the sum of them all. They are assets with a value available entirely in the short term, usually understood to be a period less than a year.

This is either because they are what the business sells, or because they are money or can quickly be turned into money. Examples of current assets are:

- stock
- money owing by customers (debtors)
- money in the bank
- short-term investments.

SUNDAY
MONDAY
TUESDAY
WEDNESDAY
THURSDAY
FRIDAY
SATURDAY

Current liabilities

These too are listed separately in the Balance Sheet with one total given for the sum of them all. They are liabilities which the business could be called upon to pay off in the short term, usually within a year. Examples are a bank overdraft and money owing to suppliers (creditors).

Definitions of debtors and creditors

- A debtor is a person owing money to the business (e.g. a customer for goods delivered).
- A creditor is a person to whom the business owes money (e.g. an unpaid electricity bill).

Working capital

This is the difference between current assets and current liabilities. In the simple example given earlier it is £1,500.

It is extremely important as we will see later in the week. A business without sufficient working capital cannot pay its debts as they fall due. In this situation it might have to stop trading, even if it is profitable.

Possible alternatives might include raising more capital, taking out a long-term loan, or selling some fixed assets.

Prudent reserves

When something happens that causes an asset to lose value, it is written off. For example, if some stock is stolen, the value of stock in the Balance Sheet is reduced.

The same thing must happen if a prudent view is that an asset has lost some of its value. This happens, for example, if some of the stock is obsolete and unlikely to sell for full value. Normally the Balance Sheet will just show the reduced value, which will be explained with notes.

The creation of a stock reserve reduces the profit. If it is subsequently found that the reserve was not necessary, the asset is restored to its full value and the profit is correspondingly increased in a later period.

It is often necessary to create a bad debt reserve to cover money that may not be collectable from customers.

Test your knowledge of Balance Sheets

A Balance Sheet for Patel Brothers is given below. For the sake of brevity, taxation and the explanatory notes have been omitted.

Now test your knowledge of Balance Sheets by answering the following questions. The answers are given at the end of this chapter, immediately following the end-of-chapter questions.

1 Is the capital employed of £448,000 an asset or a liability?
2 Suggest two possible additional types of current asset.
3 What is the working capital?
4 What would the working capital be if stock valued at £10,000 was sold for £18,000 (payable after 30 days) and if an extra piece of machinery was purchased for £30,000?
5 Assume that a customer had paid a debt of £3,000 written off as bad at 31 October 2012.
  a What would the profit for the year have been?
  b What would Trade Debtors at 31 October 2012 be?

Patel Brothers
Balance Sheet at 31 October 2012

	£	£
Fixed Assets		
Freehold premises	200,000	
Fixtures and fittings	30,000	
Plant and machinery	50,000	
		280,000
Current Assets		
Stock	130,000	
Trade debtors	190,000	
Other debtors	16,000	
	336,000	
Less Current Liabilities		
Trade creditors	70,000	
Bank overdraft	48,000	
	118,000	
		218,000
Bank Loan repayable on 31/12/15		(50,000)
		448,000
Capital employed		
Capital at 31/10/11	350,000	
Add profit for year	300,000	
	650,000	
Less drawings for year	202,000	
		448,000

Summary

This Monday we have been introduced to the basic principles of the following:

- What is a Balance Sheet?
- Format of the Balance Sheet
- Elementary rules of double entry bookkeeping
- An example of a simple Balance Sheet
- Fixed assets and depreciation
- Current assets and current liabilities
- Debtors and creditors
- Working capital
- Prudent reserves

Finally, we have examined another Balance Sheet and tested our understanding of it.

Tomorrow, we will try to understand published accounts.

SUNDAY
MONDAY
TUESDAY
WEDNESDAY
THURSDAY
FRIDAY
SATURDAY

Test your knowledge of Balance Sheets – Answers

1. Liability
2. Short-term investments, bank accounts, cash
3. £218,000
4. £196,000
5.
    a) £303,000
    b) £190,000 (no change)

Fact-check (answers at the back)

1. Which words complete the following: 'The total of the debit balances must equal'?
   a) the total of the assets ☐
   b) the total of the liabilities ☐
   c) the total of the credit balances ☐
   d) the income ☐

2. The figures in the Balance Sheet reflect the position at which point in the trading period?
   a) The beginning ☐
   b) The end ☐
   c) The average ☐
   d) One week before the end ☐

3. What is not shown in a Balance Sheet?
   a) Net worth of the business ☐
   b) Fixed assets ☐
   c) Current liabilities ☐
   d) Salaries ☐

4. What are Balance Sheet liabilities? ☐
   a) Certain credit balances ☐
   b) Certain debit balances ☐
   c) Loss for the period ☐
   d) Overheads ☐

5. Where in the Balance Sheet is a bank overdraft shown?
   a) Fixed assets ☐
   b) Current assets ☐
   c) Current liabilities ☐
   d) Capital employed ☐

6. Plant and machinery cost £400,000 and depreciation to date has been £100,000. What will be shown in the Balance Sheet?

   a) £300,000 in the fixed assets ☐
   b) £300,000 in the current assets ☐
   c) £400,000 in the fixed assets ☐
   d) £100,000 in the current liabilities ☐

7. What is the period during which an asset can reasonably be expected to be turned into cash in order for it to be classed as a current asset?
   a) One month ☐
   b) Six months ☐
   c) One year ☐
   d) Two years ☐

8. What is a creditor?
   a) A director ☐
   b) A person or business to whom the business owes money ☐
   c) A person or business who owes money to the business ☐
   d) An employee who behaves in a creditable way ☐

9. What is working capital?
   a) The difference between all the assets and all the liabilities ☐
   b) All the assets ☐
   c) The employees ☐
   d) The difference between current assets and current liabilities ☐

10. What is the effect of a stock reserve?
   a) It reduces the profit ☐
   b) It increases the profit ☐
   c) It increases the current liabilities ☐
   d) It reduces the fixed assets ☐

TUESDAY

Understanding published accounts

Today, we will be studying published accounts and it will be helpful if you obtain a set of accounts. The accounts will be particularly useful if they are for a company well known to you, such as your employer. Advice on how to get hold of published accounts is given in the first section of today's work.

A study of published accounts cannot help but be interesting and useful. One of the reasons is that it will help you understand your investments and help you decide whether to buy or sell. You may think that you do not have investments but you very probably do, perhaps through the medium of a pension fund or a share-based ISA. Another possible reason is to help judge the security of your employer or prospective employer. Published accounts, of course, have many other uses and, short of fraud, much information must be disclosed and cannot be hidden.

Today's programme is perhaps the most demanding in the book. It includes:

- availability of published accounts
- what is included
- profit and Loss Account and Balance Sheet
- the remainder of the Annual Report and Accounts.

Availability of published accounts

Accounts are published for one or both of the following reasons:

- because it is required by law
- as a public relations exercise.

All but a tiny number of registered UK companies are required by law to produce accounts annually, although, subject to strict limits the period can be changed. In many cases an audit is required. A private company must file accounts at Companies House within nine months of the balance sheet date and a public company must do so within six months of the balance sheet date. An extension of the filing period may be allowed in rare and exceptional cases. The law and accounting standards stipulate the minimum content and standard of the accounts.

Certain bodies other than companies are also required to produce accounts. Examples are building societies, charities and local authorities. Our work today deals exclusively with the accounts of companies.

Companies House

The address for companies registered in England and Wales is *Companies House, Cardiff CF14 3UZ.* There is an office in Edinburgh for companies registered in Scotland and an office in Belfast for companies registered in Northern Ireland. The telephone number for all three offices is *0303 1234 500* and the website for all three offices is www.companieshouse.gov.uk. There are over 2,500,000 live companies on the register and the accounts of all but a handful of them may be inspected.

How to obtain published accounts

A listed public company will probably be willing to make accounts available. A request should be made to the Company Secretary's department.

Alternatively, you can get the accounts of any company, even the corner shop, by applying to Companies House. You can also get a copy of the company's annual return, articles and other documents. You will need to give the company's exact registered name or its registered number, preferably both. You can telephone and have the document posted to you or do it through the website. There is a charge of £3 per document if it is posted or £1 per document if it is sent electronically. You can pay with a credit or debit card. It may be useful and particularly interesting if you look at the accounts of your employer or another company that you know well.

Late filing

Unfortunately, a small minority of companies file their accounts late or even not at all. This is an offence for which the directors can be punished and the company incur a penalty, but it does happen. It is often companies with problems that file late.

What is included

The content of the Annual Report and Accounts is governed by the law and accounting standards, though directors do still have some discretion. Listed companies are required to use international accounting standards, whereas other companies can use international accounting standards or UK accounting standards. However, once international standards have been used a company can only go back to UK standards in exceptional circumstances. Which set of accounting standards is used makes a difference, both to the presentation and to the figures.

If you are looking at the Report and Accounts of a listed company you will see the following:

- Independent Auditors' Report
- Balance Sheet (it might be called Statement of Financial Position)
- Statement of Comprehensive Income or it might be called Income Statement (this corresponds with the Profit and Loss Account)
- Statement of Changes in Equity
- Statement of Cash Flows
- notes to the financial statements
- Chairman's Statement

- Directors' Report
- Business Review
- Directors' Remuneration Report.

If the company is using UK standards, the financial information will comprise:

- Balance Sheet
- Profit and Loss Account
- Statement of Total Recognized Gains and Losses
- probably a Cash Flow Statement
- notes to the financial statements.

Reports will be filed with this financial information.

Medium-sized companies (up to £25,900,000 turnover subject to conditions) may file abbreviated accounts, and small companies (up to £6,500,000 turnover subject to conditions) may file still less detail. Subject to conditions an audit is not compulsory for small companies.

Space here is limited and there is so much detail that there is really no substitute for diving in and having a look at the Report and Accounts of your chosen company. Try not to get bogged down and I wish you the best of luck. Assuming that you are not looking at the Report and Accounts of a small or medium-sized company and assuming that the company uses UK accounting standards, can you locate the following?

- the pre-tax profit (Profit and Loss Account)
- details of the fixed assets (Balance Sheet and supporting notes)
- the amount of any exports (the notes)
- is it an unqualified audit report? (the Audit Report)
- details of any political or charitable donation (the Directors' Report)
- was there a cash outflow in the period? (the Cash Flow Statement)
- details of the share capital (Balance Sheet and supporting notes)
- the amount of the capital employed (the Balance Sheet).

Profit and Loss Account and Balance Sheet

These are the core of the accounts and we have already looked at some of the principles on Sunday and Monday. The Profit and Loss Account will give the figures for the previous period as well as the current period. Figures in the Balance Sheet will be given as at the previous Balance Sheet date as well as for the present one.

Now we will have a look at what will be shown in the published Profit and Loss Account and Balance Sheet of a company and once again UK accounting standards are assumed. Some of the information may be given in notes with a suitable cross-reference.

Profit and Loss Account

Most people consider that the key figure is the one for Profit before Tax. You may think that taxation is fair, or at any rate inevitable, and that Profit before Tax is the best measure of the company's success. The bottom part of the Profit and Loss Account will look rather like this. Fictitious figures have been inserted.

Profit before Tax	£10,000,000
Less Tax on Profit	£3,200,000
Profit for the Year	£6,800,000
Less Dividends Paid and Proposed	£4,000,000
Retained Profit for the Year	£2,800,000
Retained Profit brought forward	£7,000,000
Retained Profit carried forward	£9,800,000

In this example Her Majesty's Government is taking £3,200,000 of the profit and £4,000,000 is being distributed to shareholders. The company started the current period with undistributed profits of £7,000,000 and it is prudently adding £2,800,000 to this figure. Undistributed profits are now £9,800,000 and this figure will appear in the Balance Sheet.

The Profit and Loss Account will give the turnover, which is the total invoiced sales in the period. This is very important and it is useful to work out the relationship between the profit and the turnover.

Balance Sheet

Fixed assets are normally the first item appearing in the Balance Sheet. Usually you will see just one figure for the net amount of the fixed assets and a cross-reference to a note. This note will:

- break down the assets by type
- give cumulative expenditure for each type
- give cumulative depreciation for each type
- give net asset value for each type
- state the depreciation policy for each type.

The fixed assets are usually one of the most interesting sections of the accounts. This is because it is rare for the assets to be worth exactly the figure shown.

Depreciation, according to accounting rules, rarely reflects the real-life situation, especially in times of inflation. One wonders what would be the book value of St Paul's Cathedral if the Church of England had followed depreciation rules at the time of Sir Christopher Wren.

In practice, companies sometimes revalue property assets though not usually other assets. Asset strippers specialize in buying undervalued companies then selling the fixed assets for more than book value. This is one of the reasons why the details, which will be in the notes, are so important.

Current assets and current liabilities

First the current assets will be listed by type and a total of the current assets will be given. Then the current liabilities will be listed by type and the total of the current liabilities will be given.

The difference between the two figures will be stated and this is the *net current assets* or the *working capital*. A problem is usually indicated if the current assets are smaller than the current liabilities or only slightly larger.

The assets and liabilities will be cross-referenced to notes giving appropriate details such as the following:

- a breakdown of stocks into finished goods and work in progress
- a split of debtors between trade debtors (customers) and other debtors
- details of the different types of creditor.

Capital and reserves

On Monday we examined the net worth of an organization shown at the bottom of its Balance Sheet. This section is the net worth of the company.

If the company were to be solvent and wound up, ignoring the costs of the winding up and in the unlikely event of all the assets and liabilities realizing exact book value, the total of this section is the amount that would be distributed to shareholders.

A note will give details of the different types of share capital if there are more than one. It will also give the figures for the different types of reserves, and the retained figure in the Profit and Loss Account.

The remainder of the Annual Report and Accounts

Notes to the Accounts

There are always notes to the Profit and Loss Account and Balance Sheet. Their purpose is to give further details, and they are in the form of notes to prevent the accounts getting horribly detailed and complicated. Many of the notes give a breakdown of such figures as stock and debtors.

The notes also state the accounting policies and conventions used in the preparation of the accounts. These are extremely important because these policies can greatly affect the figures. An example of such a policy would be to value stocks at the lower of cost and net realizable value. Any change to this policy could greatly affect the profit figure.

The Directors' Report

The directors are required by law to provide certain information. This includes, for example, the amount of directors' remuneration and details of any political or charitable contributions. This information is disclosed in the Directors' Report.

Cash Flow Statement

There are sometimes disputes about the figures in the Profit and Loss Account and Balance Sheet. This is one reason why cash is so important. Cash is much more a matter of fact rather than of opinion. It is either there or it is not there.

Where the cash came from (banks, shareholders, customers) is also a matter of fact. So too is where the cash went to (dividends, wages, suppliers, etc.). The Cash Flow Statement gives all this information.

The Auditor's Report

The law requires company accounts to be audited by a person or firm holding one of the approved qualifications.

Subject to certain conditions no audit is required if annual turnover is less than £6,500,000. The auditors will state whether in their opinion the accounts give a true and fair view. They do not certify the accuracy of the figures, a point which is often misunderstood.

If the auditors have reservations, they will give reasons for their concern.

Serious qualifications are rare, partly because it is in the interests of directors that they be avoided. Technical, and less serious, qualifications are more common. It is a matter of judgement how seriously each one is regarded.

Consolidated Accounts

A large group may have a hundred or more companies. It would obviously give an incomplete picture if each of these companies gave information just about its own activities. This is especially true when companies in a group trade with each other.

This is why the holding company must include consolidated accounts as well as its own figures. The effect of inter-group trading is eliminated and the Consolidated Balance Sheet gives the group's position in relation to the outside world. This does not, however, remove the obligation for every group company to prepare and file its own accounts. Such accounts must include the name, in the opinion of the directors, of the ultimate holding company.

Summary

Today we have:

- Examined the obligation to publish accounts and seen where copies can be obtained
- Seen what is included in the Annual Report and Accounts
- Tested our knowledge
- Conducted an outline study of the Annual Report and Accounts

Tomorrow, we will go on to look at accounting ratios and investment decisions.

SUNDAY

MONDAY

TUESDAY

WEDNESDAY

THURSDAY

FRIDAY

SATURDAY

Fact-check (answers at the back)

1. Where is the Companies House for companies registered in Scotland located?
   - a) London ❑
   - b) Cardiff ❑
   - c) Edinburgh ❑
   - d) Glasgow ❑

2. Which bodies do not have to make published accounts generally available?
   - a) Building societies ❑
   - b) Registered charities ❑
   - c) Local authorities ❑
   - d) General partnerships ❑

3. How much does Companies House charge for providing a company's accounts electronically?
   - a) £1 ❑
   - b) £2 ❑
   - c) £5 ❑
   - d) £20 ❑

4. To what extent must listed companies use international accounting standards?
   - a) Always ❑
   - b) Usually ❑
   - c) Always unless special permission is obtained ❑
   - d) Never ❑

5. What is the turnover limit (subject to conditions) for the filing of abbreviated accounts for small companies at Companies House?
   - a) £1,000,000 ❑
   - b) £5,000,000 ❑
   - c) £6,500,000 ❑
   - d) £7,500,000 ❑

6. Which document explains the change in the amount of cash?
   - a) The Balance Sheet ❑
   - b) The Statement of Cash Flows ❑
   - c) The Directors' Report ❑
   - d) The Independent Auditors' Report ❑

7. Which document gives details of any charitable donations?
   - a) The Profit and Loss Account ❑
   - b) The Directors' Report ❑
   - c) The Balance Sheet ❑
   - d) The Cash Flow Statement ❑

8. What does the auditor do?
   - a) Give an opinion ❑
   - b) Certify the figures ❑
   - c) Prepare the accounts ❑
   - d) Comment on whether the directors are being fairly paid ❑

9. How many companies in the UK send accounts to Companies House?
   - a) More then 50,000 ❑
   - b) More than 1,000,000 ❑
   - c) More than 2,000,000 ❑
   - d) More than 2,500,000 ❑

10. Must a Business Review be provided in the Report and Accounts of a listed company?
    - a) Yes, always ❑
    - b) Usually ❑
    - c) Sometimes ❑
    - d) No ❑

WEDNESDAY

Accounting ratios and investment decisions

So far we have studied accounts and what they mean. Now we will devote a day to the active use of financial information. First we will take a look at ratios in the accounts, and then move on to investment decisions. Today is far from the easiest day but, provided that you have mastered the basics, it should be one of the most interesting and rewarding.

The programme includes:

- accounting ratios
- four key questions
- testing our understanding of accounting ratios
- investment decisions.

Accounting ratios

There are many useful ratios that can be taken from accounts.
The following are among the most important but there are
many others. It is a good idea to have a set of accounts with
you as you work through this section. Pick out relevant figures,
work out the ratios, and try to draw conclusions.

Profit to turnover

For example:

Annual turnover	**£10,000,000**
Annual profit before tax	**£1,000,000**
Profit to turnover	**10%**

This uses Profit before Tax but it may be more useful to use
Profit after Tax. Perhaps you want to define profit as excluding
the charge for bank interest. You should select the definition
most relevant to your circumstances. The ratio may be
expressed in different ways (e.g. 1 to 10 instead of 10%).

Return on capital employed

For example:

Capital employed	£5,000,000
Annual profit after tax	£1,000,000
Return on capital employed	20%

Again the profit may be expressed before or after tax.

Capital employed is the net amount invested in the business by the owners and is taken from the Balance Sheet. Many people consider this the most important ratio of all. It is useful to compare the result with a return that can be obtained outside the business. If a building society is paying a higher rate, perhaps the business should be closed down and the money put in the building society.

Note that there are two ways of improving the return. In the example, the return on capital employed would be 25% if the profit was increased to £1,250,000. It would also be 25% if the capital employed was reduced to £4,000,000.

Stock turn

For example:

Annual turnover	£10,000,000
Annual cost of sales (60%)	£6,000,000
Stock value	£1,500,000
Stock turn	4

As the name implies, this measures the number of times that total stock is used (turned over) in the course of a year. The higher the stock turn the more efficiently the business is being run, though adequate safety margins must of course be maintained.

It is important that the terms are completely understood and that there are no abnormal factors. Normally the definition of stock includes all finished goods, work in progress and raw materials.

The stock value will usually be taken from the closing Balance Sheet but you need to consider if it is a typical figure. If the business is seasonal, such as a manufacturer of fireworks, it may not be. A better result may be obtained if the average of several stock figures throughout the year can be used.

Number of days' credit granted

For example:

Annual turnover including VAT	**£10,000,000**
Trade debtors	**£1,500,000**
Number of days' credit	**55**

The calculation is $\dfrac{1,500,000}{10,000,000} \times 365 = 55$ days

Obviously the lower the number of days the more efficiently the business is being run. The figure for trade debtors normally comes from the closing Balance Sheet and care should be taken that it is a figure typical of the whole year.

If £1,500,000 of the £10,000,000 turnover came in the final month, the number of days' credit is really 31 instead of 55. Care should also be taken that the VAT-inclusive debtors figure is compared with the VAT-inclusive turnover figure. VAT is normally excluded from the Profit and Loss Account.

Number of days' credit taken

The principle of the calculation is exactly the same. In this case the figure for closing trade creditors is compared with that for the annual purchases.

Gearing

The purpose of this ratio is to compare the finance provided by the banks and other borrowing with the finance invested by shareholders. It is a ratio much used by banks, who may not like to see a ratio of 1 to 1 (or some other such proportion) exceeded.The ratio is sometimes expressed as a proportion, as in 1 to 1. Sometimes it is expressed as a percentage: 1 to 1 is 50% because borrowing is 50% of the total. Gearing is said to be high when borrowing is high in relation to shareholders' funds. This can be dangerous but shareholders' returns will be high if the company does well. This is what is meant by being highly geared.

For example:

Loans	**£6,000,000**
Shareholders' funds	**£3,000,000**
Gearing	**200%**

Dividend per share

This is the total dividends for the year divided by the number of shares in issue. Any preference shares are normally disregarded.

For example:

Total dividends	**£2,000,000**
Number of issued shares	**10,000,000**
Dividend per share	**20p**

Price/earnings ratio

This is one of the most helpful of the investment ratios and it can be used to compare different companies. The higher the number the more expensive the shares. It is often useful to do the calculation based on anticipated future earnings rather than declared historic earnings, although of course you can never be certain what future earnings will be.

The calculation is the current quoted price per share divided by earnings per share.

For example:

Profit after tax	**£5,000,000**
Number of issued shares	**10,000,000**
Earnings per share	**50p**
Current share price	**£7.50**
Price/earnings ratio	**15**

For all the ratios, if you have access to frequently produced management accounts the ratios will be more useful.

Before leaving accounting ratios please take warning from a true story. Some years ago one of the accountancy bodies asked examination candidates to work with ratios and draw conclusions from a Balance Sheet given in the examination paper.

Many of the students said that the company was desperately short of working capital and predicted imminent trouble. They were badly mistaken because the Balance Sheet had been taken from the latest published accounts of Marks and Spencer PLC. The students had not spotted the possibilities that the sales were for cash, the purchases were on credit and the business was very well managed.

Four key questions

There are many traps in using financial information and interpreting accounting ratios. You are advised to approach the job with caution and always to keep in mind four key questions.

Am I comparing like with like?

Financial analysts pay great attention to the notes in accounts and to the stated accounting policies. One of the reasons for this is that changes in accounting policies can affect the figures and hence the comparisons.

Consider a company that writes off research and development costs as overheads as soon as they are incurred. Then suppose that it changes policy and decides to capitalize the research and development, holding it in the Balance Sheet as having a long-term value. A case can be made for either treatment but the change makes it difficult to compare ratios for different years.

Is there an explanation?

Do not forget that there may be a special reason for an odd-looking ratio.

For example, greetings card manufacturers commonly deliver Christmas cards in August with an arrangement that payment is due on 1 January. The 30 June Balance Sheet may show that customers are taking an average of 55 days' credit. The 31 December Balance Sheet may show that customers are taking an average of 120 days' credit.

This does not mean that the position has deteriorated dreadfully and the company is in trouble. The change in the period of credit is an accepted feature of the trade and happens every year. It is of course important, particularly as extra working capital has to be found at the end of each year.

What am I comparing it with?

A ratio by itself has only limited value. It needs to be compared with something. Useful comparisons may be with the company budget, last year's ratio, or competitors' ratios.

Do I believe the figures?

You may be working with audited and published figures. On the other hand, you may only have unchecked data rushed from the accountant's desk. This sort of information may be more valuable because it is up to date. But beware of errors. Even if you are not a financial expert, if it feels wrong, perhaps it is wrong.

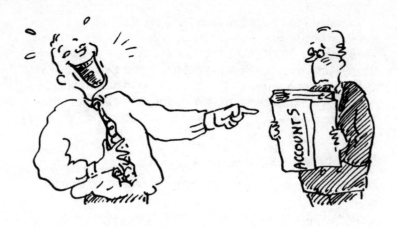

Test your understanding of accounting ratios

The Balance Sheet of Bristol Adhesives Ltd follows. The following information is available for the year to 31 October 2012.

Turnover was	*£6,600,000*
Profit before Tax was	*£66,000*
The bank overdraft limit is	*£800,000*
Cost of sales was	*50%*

1 What was the ratio of Profit to Turnover?
2 What was the Return on Capital Employed?
3 What was the Stock Turn?
4 What was the number of days' credit granted? (Ignore possible VAT implications.)
5
   a What is the working capital?
   b Does this give cause for concern?

Answers are given after the end-of-chapter questions.

Bristol Adhesives Ltd

Balance Sheet at 31 October 2012

	£	£
Fixed Assets		2,000,000
Current Assets		
Stock	1,800,000	
Trade debtors	700,000	
Other debtors	300,000	
	2,800,000	
Less Current Liabilities		
Trade creditors	1,400,000	
Bank overdraft	800,000	
Other creditors	400,000	
	2,600,000	
Net Current Assets		200,000
		2,200,000
Capital and Reserves		
Called-up share capital		1,500,000
Profit and Loss Account		700,000
		2,200,000

Investment decisions

Some investment decisions are easy to make. Perhaps
a government safety regulation makes an item of capital
expenditure compulsory. Or perhaps an essential piece of
machinery breaks down and just has to be replaced.

Many other investment decisions are not nearly so clear
cut and hinge on whether the proposed expenditure will
generate sufficient future cash savings to justify itself.
There are many very sophisticated techniques for aiding this
decision, but today we will look at three techniques that are
commonly used.

Payback

This has the merit of being extremely simple to calculate and understand. It is a simple measure of the period of time taken for the savings made to equal the capital expenditure. For example:

A new machine will cost £100,000. It will save £40,000 running expenses in the first year and £30,000 per year after that.

The payback period would be three years because this is the time taken for the saving on costs to equal the original expenditure. Hopefully this only took you a few seconds to work out and it is very useful information to have.

The disadvantage of the payback technique is that no account is given to the value of holding money. The £30,000 saved in year 3 is given equal value to £30,000 of the £100,000 paid out on day 1. In fact, inflation and loss of interest mean that, in reality, it is less valuable.

Return on investment

This takes the average of the money saved over the life of the asset and expresses it as a percentage of the original sum invested. For example:

A new machine will cost £100,000 and have a life of eight years. It will save £40,000 running expenses in the first year, and £30,000 in each of the remaining seven years.

The return on investment is $\frac{250,000 \times 100}{100,000 \times 8} = 31.25\%$ p.a.

Return on investment, like payback, takes no account of the time factor. A pound in eight years' time is given equal value with a pound today.

Discounted cash flow

This technique takes account of the fact that money paid or received in the future is not as valuable as money paid or received now. For this reason it is considered superior to payback and to return on investment. However, it is not as simple to calculate and understand.

There are variations to the discounted cash flow technique but the principles are illustrated by the following example.

The purchase of two competing pieces of machinery is under consideration. Machine A costs £100,000 and will save £60,000 in year 1 and £55,000 in year 2. Machine B costs £90,000 and will save £55,000 in both year 1 and year 2. The savings are taken to occur at the end of each year and the company believes that the money saved will earn 10% p.a. in bank interest.

The calculations are:

	Machine A	Machine B
Expenditure now	£100,000	£90,000
Less year 1 savings (discounted)	£54,600	£50,050
	£45,400	£39,950
Less year 2 savings (discounted)	£45,650	£45,650
Savings at Net Present Value	£250	£5,700

The example has of course been unrealistically simplified. However, it shows that after bringing the future values back to Net Present Value, Machinery B is the better purchase.

Summary

Today, we have looked at how financial information is actively used and specifically at:

- Useful accounting ratios
- Four possible reasons for caution
- Our understanding of accounting ratios
- Financial techniques aiding investment decisions

Tomorrow, we shall go on to increase our understanding of cash and the management of working capital.

SUNDAY

MONDAY

TUESDAY

WEDNESDAY

THURSDAY

FRIDAY

SATURDAY

Test your understanding of accounting ratios – Answers

1. 66,000/6,600,000 = 1%
2. 66,000/2,200,000 = 3%
3. 3,300,000/1,800,000 = 1.8
4. 700,000/6,600,000 x 365 = 39 days
5.
   a) £200,000
   b) Yes (cause for further enquiry anyway)

Fact-check (answers at the back)

The following information is taken from a Profit and Loss Account, Balance Sheet and other sources. Please use it to answer the first seven questions.

Turnover for year (excluding VAT)	£100,000,000
Turnover for year (including VAT)	£120,000,000
Profit after tax for year	£6,000,000
Capital employed (shareholders' funds)	£40,000,000
Loans	£50,000,000
Cost of sales for year	£50,000,000
Stock	£10,000,000
Trade debtors	£20,000,000
Dividends paid and proposed	£4,000,000
Number of shares in issue	10,000,000
Current share price	£6.00

1. What is the ratio for profit to turnover (excluding VAT)?
   a) 10% ☐
   b) 5% ☐
   c) 6% ☐
   d) 20% ☐

2. What is the return on capital employed?
   a) 10% ☐
   b) 12% ☐
   c) 15% ☐
   d) 20% ☐

3. What is the stock turn?
   a) 4 ☐
   b) 5 ☐
   c) 6 ☐
   d) 7 ☐

4. What are the number of days' credit taken by customers?
   a) 55 days ☐
   b) 60 days ☐
   c) 61 days ☐
   d) 64 days ☐

5. What is the gearing?
   a) 50% ☐
   b) 80% ☐
   c) 100% ☐
   d) 125% ☐

6. What is the dividend per share?
   a) 20p ☐
   b) 40p ☐
   c) 60p ☐
   d) 80p ☐

7. What is the price/earnings ratio?
   a) 10.0 ☐
   b) 10.5 ☐
   c) 11.0 ☐
   d) 11.5 ☐

8. A new machine will cost £500,000 and will save £200,000 running expenses for each of five years. What is the payback period?

a) 24 months ❏
b) 30 months ❏
c) 36 months ❏
d) 60 months ❏

9. A new computer system will cost £80,000 and have a life of four years and it will then be scrapped. It will save £50,000 per year. What is the return on investment?

a) 60.0% ❏
b) 62.5% ❏
c) 65.0% ❏
d) 67.5% ❏

10. Which of the following (in the opinion of many people) makes discounted cash flow superior to return on investment? The other three statements are not true.

a) It is easier to calculate ❏
b) It is a legal requirement ❏
c) It is recommended by the European Union ❏
d) It takes account of the changing value of money ❏

THURSDAY

Cash and the management of working capital

It is a bad mistake to underestimate the importance of cash and it is another bad mistake to confuse cash and profit. They can be very different and the reasons are explained in this chapter. It is sometimes said that 'Cash is King'. The origins of the saying are not beyond doubt but the words are often attributed to Jim Slater. He was the financier of Slater Walker fame who, in his words, became a minus millionaire, but went on to recover much of his fortune.

Today we look at the importance and management of cash. We also look at the management of working capital and the place of cash within it.

The programme comprises:

- the distinctions between profit and cash
- what is cash?
- the Cash-Flow Forecast
- the management of working capital.

The distinctions between profit and cash

Cash is completely different from profit, a fact that is not always properly appreciated. It is possible, and indeed quite common, for a business to be profitable but short of cash. Among the differences are the following:

- Money may be collected from customers more slowly (or more quickly) than money is paid to suppliers.
- Capital expenditure (unless financed by hire purchase or similar means) has an immediate impact on cash. The effect on profit, by means of depreciation, is spread over a number of years.
- Taxation, dividends and other payments to owners are an appropriation of profit. Cash is taken out of the business, which may be more or less than the profit.

- An expanding business will have to spend money on materials, items for sale, wages, etc. before it completes the extra sales and gets paid. Purchases and expenses come first. Sales and profit come later.

It is worth illustrating the problems of an expanding business with a hypothetical but realistic example.

Company A manufactures pens. It has a regular monthly turnover of £20,000. The cost of the pens is £10,000 (50%). Other monthly costs are £8,000 and its monthly profit is £2,000.

At 31 December, Company A has £3,000 in the bank and is owed £40,000 by customers to whom it allows two months' credit.

It owes £15,000 to suppliers who are paid within 30 days. Monthly costs of £3,000 are payable in cash.

The company secures an additional order for £60,000. The extra pens will take two months to make and will be delivered on 28 February. The customer will then have 60 days to pay.

The cost of the additional pens will be £30,000 (50%) and there will be extra expenses of £14,000 in the two months. The new order will contribute a very satisfactory £16,000 extra profit.

By 30 April, Company A will have made £24,000 profit. This is the regular £2,000 a month plus the £16,000 from the additional order.

Now let us assume that the new customer pays on 1 May, just one day late. Despite the extra profit, on 30 April the £3,000 bank balance will have turned into a £33,000 overdraft. The calculation is as follows:

Balance at 31 December	£3,000
Add receipts in four months	£80,000
	£83,000
Less payments to creditors in four months	£90,000
	(£7,000)
Less cash expenses in four months	£26,000
Overdraft at 30 April	(£33,000)

What is cash?

Cash includes the notes and coins in the petty cash box. It also includes money in bank current accounts, and money in various short-term investment accounts that can quickly be turned into available cash.

It is common for a Balance Sheet to show only a tiny amount for cash. This is because the business has an overdraft and only such things as the petty cash are included.

Practical management usage of the term cash includes a negative figure for an overdraft. A Cash-Flow Forecast can often result in a series of forecast overdrafts.

The Cash-Flow Forecast

It is extremely important that cash receipts and payments are effectively planned and anticipated. This has not been done in nearly all businesses that fail. A good manager will plan that sufficient resources are available but that not too many resources are tied up.

This can be done in isolation but it is better done as part of the overall budgeting process. Budgets are examined on Saturday.

The preparation of a detailed Cash-Flow Forecast will yield many benefits. Calculating and writing down the figures may suggest ideas as to how they can be improved. For example, the figures for cash payments from trade debtors will be based on an estimate of the average number of days' credit that will be taken. This will pose the question of whether or not payments can be speeded up.

When the Cash-Flow Forecast is finished it will be necessary to consider if the results are acceptable. Even if resources are available the results might not be satisfactory, and improvements will have to be worked out.

If sufficient resources are not available, either changes must be made or extra resources arranged. Perhaps an additional bank overdraft can be negotiated. Either way, a well-planned document will help managers to take action in good time.

The principles of a Cash-Flow Forecast are best illustrated with an example and a good one is given in the following table.

Variations in the layout are possible but a constant feature should be the running cash or overdraft balance.

Do not overlook contingencies and do not overlook the possibility of a peak figure within a period. For example, Ace Toys Ltd are forecast to have £17,000 on 31 March and £5,000 on 30 April. Both forecasts could be exactly right and the company still need a £15,000 overdraft on 15 April.

Ace Toys Ltd – Cash-Flow Forecast for half year

	January £000	February £000	March £000	April £000	May £000	June £000
Receipts						
UK customers	50	55	55	55	60	80
Export customers	20	20	20	20	25	20
All other	5	5	8	2	12	6
	75	80	83	77	97	106
Payments						
Purchase ledger suppliers	30	33	29	40	44	38
Wages (net)	14	13	13	17	13	13
PAYE and National Insurance	4	4	4	4	5	4
Corporation tax	–	–	30	–	–	–
Capital expenditure	7	4	25	20	2	2
All other	8	9	9	8	6	11
	63	63	110	89	70	68
Excess of Receipts over Payments	12	17	(27)	(12)	27	38
Add Opening Bank Balance	15	27	44	17	5	32
Closing Bank Balance	27	44	17	5	32	70

74

It will help fix the principles in your mind if you now prepare your own personal Cash-Flow forecast. Set it out in accordance with the format illustrated below.

The figures will be smaller but the principles are identical. Most people have never done this and the results may well be revealing. The opening bank balance in month 1 should be the latest figure on your personal bank statement.

	Month 1	Month 2	Month 3
	£	£	£
Receipts			
Salary			
Interest			
Dividends			
Other (specify)			
Payments			
Mortgage or rent			
Telephone			
Gas and electricity			
Food			
Car expenses			
Other (specify)			
Excess of Receipts over Payments			
Add Opening Bank Balance			
Closing Bank Balance			

The management of working capital

Is it important?

The effective management of working capital can be critical to the survival of the business and it is hard to think of anything more important than that. Many businesses that fail are profitable at the time of their failure, and failure often comes as a surprise to the managers. The reason for the failure is a shortage of working capital.

Furthermore, effective management of working capital is likely to improve profitability significantly. Turn back to Wednesday's section on return on capital employed. You will remember that the percentage return increases as capital employed is reduced. Effective management of working capital can reduce the capital employed. It increases profits as well as enabling managers to sleep soundly without worries.

The four largest elements affecting working capital are usually debtors, stock, creditors and cash. Success in managing the first three affect cash, which can be reinvested in the business or distributed. We will consider the three elements in turn.

Debtors

British business is plagued by slow payment of invoices and it is a problem in many other countries, too. Most businesses, and the government, would like to see an improvement. A statutory right to interest has been in place for a number of years but nothing seems to make much difference. An improvement can significantly affect working capital.

It is a great problem for managers, who sometimes are frightened of upsetting customers and feel that there is little that they can do. This is completely the wrong attitude.

Customer relations must always be considered, but a great deal can be done. Some practical steps for credit control are summarized below:

- Have the right attitude; ask early and ask often.
- Make sure that payment terms are agreed in advance.
- Do not underestimate the strength of your position.
- Give credit control realistic status and priority.
- Have well-thought out credit policies.
- Concentrate on the biggest and most worrying debts first.
- Be efficient; send out invoices and statements promptly.
- Deal with queries quickly and efficiently.
- Make full use of the telephone, your best aid.
- Use legal action if necessary.

This may sound obvious, but it usually works. To sum up: be efficient, ask and be tough if necessary.

Stock

The aim should be to keep stock as low as is realistically feasible, and to achieve as high a rate of stock turnover as is realistically feasible. In practice, it is usually necessary to compromise between the wish to have stock as low as possible, and the need to keep production and sales going with a reasonable margin of safety.

Exactly how the compromise is struck will vary from case to case. Purchasing and production control are highly skilled functions and great effort may be expended on getting it right.

You may be familiar with the phrase 'just in time deliveries'. This is the technique of arranging deliveries of supplies frequently and in small quantities. In fact, just in time to keep production going. It is particularly successful in Japan where, for example, car manufacturers keep some parts for production measured only in hours.

It is not easy to achieve and suppliers would probably like to make large deliveries at irregular intervals. It may pay to approach the problem with an attitude of partnership with key suppliers, and to reward them with fair prices and continuity of business.

Finished goods should be sold, delivered and invoiced as quickly as possible.

Creditors

It is not ethical advice, but there is an obvious advantage in paying suppliers slowly. This is why slow payment is such a problem and, as has already been stated, the control of debtors is so important. Slow payment is often imposed by large and strong companies on small and weak suppliers.

Slow payment does not affect the net balance of working capital, but it does mean that both cash and creditors are higher than would otherwise be the case. Apart from moral considerations, there are some definite disadvantages in a policy of slow payment:

- Suppliers will try to compensate with higher prices or lower service.
- Best long-term results are often obtained by fostering mutual loyalty with key suppliers; it pays to consider their interests.
- If payments are already slow, there will be less scope for taking longer to pay in response to a crisis.

For these reasons it is probably not wise to adopt a consistent policy of slow payment, at least with important suppliers. It is better to be hard but fair, and to ensure that this fair play is rewarded with keen prices, good service and perhaps prompt payment discounts.

There may be scope for timing deliveries to take advantage of payment terms. For example if the terms are 'net monthly account', a 30 June delivery will be due for payment on 31 July. A 1 July delivery will be due for payment on 31 August.

Summary

Today we have:

- Studied the distinctions between profit and cash
- Examined an example illustrating the differences
- Seen what is meant by the term 'cash'
- Looked at Cash-Flow Forecasts
- Studied the importance of working capital and looked closely at debtors, stock and creditors

Tomorrow, we will continue by taking a look at costing.

SUNDAY

MONDAY

TUESDAY

WEDNESDAY

THURSDAY

FRIDAY

SATURDAY

Fact-check (answers at the back)

1. 'A business may be profitable but short of cash'. How prevalent is this?
   a) It is relatively common ❏
   b) It is relatively uncommon ❏
   c) It is very uncommon ❏
   d) The statement in the question is self-evidently absurd ❏

2. Money is collected from customers more slowly than in the past. What effect will this have on cash in the business?
   a) There will be no effect ❏
   b) It will reduce the cash in the business ❏
   c) It will increase the cash in the business ❏
   d) It will greatly increase the cash in the business ❏

3. How important (in many people's opinion) is it that a cash-flow forecast is regularly prepared?
   a) It is a waste of time ❏
   b) It might be interesting ❏
   c) It could be useful ❏
   d) It is important ❏

4. Which of the following is not included in the definition of cash?
   a) Notes and coin in the petty cash box ❏
   b) Money in bank current accounts ❏
   c) Money owing by customers and due to be paid within three days ❏
   d) Bank overdrafts ❏

5. Which of the following statements is not true?
   a) The cash requirement in the middle of a month may be higher than the cash requirement at the beginning and end of the month ❏
   b) Capital expenditure is a cash outflow ❏
   c) The running cash or overdraft balance should always be a feature of a cash-flow forecast ❏
   d) Cash is the same as retained profit ❏

6. Which of the following will not help keep working capital at a satisfactory level?
   a) Persuade customers to pay quickly ❏
   b) Reduce dividends paid by the company ❏
   c) Change the policy on depreciating fixed assets ❏
   d) Turn over stock more quickly ❏

7. Payment terms are 'net monthly account'. When is an invoice dated 6 September due for payment?
   a) 6 September ❏
   b) 30 September ❏
   c) 6 October ❏
   d) 31 October ❏

8. Slower payment by customers has which two of the following consequences?
a) Debtors are increased ❏
b) Creditors are increased ❏
c) Cash is increased ❏
d) Cash is reduced ❏

9. What are the two ways to increase the return on capital employed?
a) Increase the profit ❏
b) Increase the fixed assets ❏
c) Reduce the capital employed ❏
d) Negotiate better terms with the bank ❏

10. Who is famous for coining the phrase 'Cash is King'?
a) Gordon Brown ❏
b) Robert Maxwell ❏
c) Jim Slater ❏
d) Richard Branson ❏

FRIDAY

Costing

It is probably true to say that most non-financial managers instinctively know that costing is important. Unfortunately it is probably also true to say that most non-financial managers do not know very much about it. This is a pity because it affects so many business decisions. To take just one example, the fact that the fixed costs of running a cruise ship do not vary (or realistically only vary slightly) according to the number of passengers is the reason that large last-minute price reductions are often available. Think of that when you book your holiday.

A basic understanding of the principles of costing is important in business management. The aim today is to master these key basic costing principles:

- the value of costing
- the uses of costing
- absorption costing
- break-even charts
- marginal costing and standard costing.

← HIDDEN COST!

The value of costing

The value of costing can be illustrated with a simple example. Consider a company with three products. Its financial accounts show sales of £1,000,000, total costs of £700,000 and a profit of £300,000. The managers think that this is very good and that no significant changes are necessary. However, the costing details disclose the following:

	Product 1 £000	Product 2 £000	Product 3 £000	Total £000
Sales	600	300	100	1,000
Fixed costs	70	60	50	180
Variable costs	280	160	80	520
Total costs	350	220	130	700
Profit contribution	250	80	(30)	300

This shows that Product 1, as well as having the biggest proportion of sales, is contributing proportionately the most profit. Despite the overall good profit, Product 3 is making a negative contribution.

The obvious reaction might be to discontinue Product 3, but this may well be a mistake: £50,000 of fixed costs would have to be allocated to the other two products and the total profit would be reduced to £280,000.

Product 3 should probably only be discontinued if the fixed costs can be cut, or if the other two products can be expanded to absorb the £50,000 fixed costs.

It is increasingly common for cost accounts to be integrated with financial accounts. If cost accounts are kept separately, they go further than financial accounts. Cost accounts break down costs to individual products and cost centres. Financial accounts are more concerned with historical information.

Much, but not all, of the information comes from the financial accounts. It is important that if cost accounts are kept separately they are reconciled with the financial accounts.

Cost accounts are much more valuable if the information can be made speedily available. Sometimes it is necessary to compromise between speed and accuracy.

The uses of costing

It costs time and money to produce costing information and it is only worth doing if the information is put to good use. The following are some of these uses.

To control costs

Possession of detailed information about costs is of obvious value in the controlling of those costs.

To promote responsibility

Management theorists agree that power and responsibility should go together, although often they do not do so. Timely and accurate costing information will help top management hold all levels of management responsible for the budgets that they control.

Care should be taken that managers are not held responsible for costs that are not within their control. As many readers will know from bitter experience, this does sometimes happen.

To aid business decisions

The case given earlier today might be such a decision.

Management must decide what to do about the unprofitable product.

To aid decisions on pricing

We live in competitive times and the old 'cost plus' contracts are now virtually never encountered. What the market will bear is usually the main factor in setting prices. Nevertheless, detailed knowledge concerning costs is an important factor in determining prices. Only in exceptional circumstances will managers agree to price goods at below cost, and they will seek to make an acceptable margin over cost.

Accurate costing is vital when tenders are submitted for major contracts and errors can have significant consequences. It is a long time ago but massive costing errors on the Millennium Dome at Greenwich were a spectacular example of what can go wrong.

Absorption costing

This takes account of all costs and allocates them to individual products or cost centres. Some costs relate directly to a product and this is quite straightforward in principle, although very detailed record-keeping may be necessary. Other costs do not relate to just one product and these must be allocated according to a fair formula. These indirect costs must be *absorbed* by each product.

There is not a single correct method of allocating overhead costs to individual products and it is sometimes right to allocate different costs in different ways. The aim should be to achieve fairness in each individual case.

Among the costs that can be entirely allocated to individual products are direct wages and associated employment costs, materials and bought-in components.

Among the costs that cannot be entirely allocated to individual products are indirect wages (cleaners, maintenance staff, etc.), wages of staff such as salesmen and accountants, and general overheads such as rent and business rates.

Great care must be taken in deciding the best way to allocate the non-direct costs. There are many different ways and the following two are common examples.

Production hours

The overhead costs are apportioned according to the direct production hours charged to each product or cost centre. For example, consider a company with just two products, A having 5,000 hours charged and B having 10,000 hours charged. If the overhead is £60,000, Product A will absorb £20,000 and Product B will absorb £40,000.

Machine hours

The principle is the same but the overhead is allocated according to the number of hours that the machinery has been running.

This is best illustrated with an example. You should try to write down the cost statement before checking the solution.

Fruit Products Ltd manufactures three types of jam. Its overhead costs in January are £18,000 and it allocates them in the proportion of direct labour costs. The following details are available for January:

	Strawberry	Raspberry	Apricot	Total
Jars manufactured	26,000	60,000	87,000	173,000
Direct labour	£2,000	£4,000	£6,000	£12,000
Ingredients	£6,000	£11,000	£17,000	£34,000
Other direct costs	£2,000	£3,000	£6,000	£11,000

The resulting cost statement is shown below:

Fruit Products Ltd – January Cost Statement

	Strawberry	Raspberry	Apricot	Total
Jars produced	26,000	60,000	87,000	173,000
	£	£	£	£
Costs				
Direct labour	2,000	4,000	6,000	12,000
Ingredients	6,000	11,000	17,000	34,000
Other direct costs	2,000	3,000	6,000	11,000
Total Direct Costs	10,000	18,000	29,000	57,000
Overhead allocation	3,000	6,000	9,000	18,000
Total Cost	13,000	24,000	38,000	75,000
Cost per jar	50.0p	40.0p	43.7p	43.4p

You will notice that in the example, direct labour is smaller than the overhead cost that is being allocated. If the overheads had been allocated in a different way, perhaps on floor area utilized, then the result would almost certainly not have been the same.

The trend in modern manufacturing is for direct costs, and particularly direct labour costs, to reduce as a proportion of the total costs. This increases the importance of choosing the fairest method of apportionment.

Break-even charts

In nearly all businesses there is a close correlation between the level of turnover and the profit or loss. The managers should know that if invoiced sales reach a certain figure the business will break even. If invoiced sales are above that figure the business will be in profit.

The break-even point depends on the relationship between the fixed and the variable costs. It is often shown in the form of the following chart:

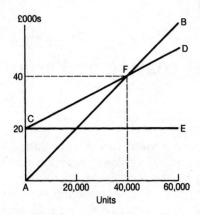

In the example, fixed costs (shown by line C–E) are £20,000. Variable costs are 50 pence per unit and the total costs (shown by line C–D) are the result of adding these to the fixed costs.

The revenue (shown by line A–B) is the result of sales at £1 per unit.

The break-even point is 40,000 units sold at £1 each. This is equal to the total cost of £40,000 (£20,000 fixed and £20,000 variable). It is at point F where the lines cross. Profit or loss can also be read from the chart.

In practice, the relationships are rarely quite so straightforward, as some of the costs may be semi-variable.

Marginal costing and standard costing

Marginal costing

Marginal costing is a useful way of emphasizing the marginal costs of production and services. This information is of great help in making pricing decisions.

If the selling price is less than the variable cost (direct cost), the loss will increase as more units are sold. Managers will only want to do this in very exceptional circumstances, such as a supermarket selling baked beans as a loss leader.

If the selling price is greater than the variable cost, then the margin will absorb part of the fixed cost. After a certain point profits will be made. Marginal costing explains why some goods and services are sold very cheaply. It explains, for example, why airline tickets are sometimes available at extremely low prices for last-minute purchasers.

Once an airline is committed to making a flight, an extremely high part of the cost of that flight can properly be regarded as a fixed cost. The pilot's salary will be the same whether the plane is empty or full. The variable cost is only the complimentary meals and a few other items. It therefore makes sense to make last-minute sales of unsold seats at low prices. As long as the selling price is greater than the variable cost, a contribution is made.

Standard costing

Standard costing involves the setting of targets, or standards, for the different factors affecting costs. Variances from the standard are then studied in detail.

For example:

Standard timber usage per unit of production	4.00 metres
Standard timber price	£2.00 per metre
Actual production	3,500 posts
Actual timber usage	14,140 metres
Actual cost of timber used	£27,714

Material Price Variance is (£28,280 less £27,714)	£566 favourable (2%)
Material Usage Variance is ([14,140 metres less 14,000 metres] x £2)	£280 adverse (1%)

The material price variance happens because the standard cost of the 14,140 metres used was £28,280 (at £2 per metre). The actual cost was £27,714, a favourable variance of £566. On the other hand, 140 metres of timber too much was used, resulting in an adverse material usage variance.

Summary

Costing is a big subject and there is only space to set out some of the basic principles. However, today we should have:

- Formed an understanding of the concept of costing
- Formed an understanding of the uses and value of costing
- Studied the principles of absorption costing
- Examined break-even charts
- Answered the basic question 'What is marginal costing?'
- Answered the basic question 'What is standard costing?'

Tomorrow, we will finish our examination of finance with a look at budgets.

SUNDAY MONDAY TUESDAY WEDNESDAY THURSDAY FRIDAY SATURDAY

Fact-check (answers at the back)

1. Which of the following is not one of the possible uses of costing information?
   a) To control costs ❑
   b) To ensure that the trial balance balances ❑
   c) To aid business decisions ❑
   d) To aid decisions on pricing ❑

2. What should happen if the cost accounts are kept separately from the financial accounts? There could be at least a tenuous case for all of the following but one of them is particularly important
   a) They should be kept in the same building ❑
   b) They should be reconciled with the financial accounts ❑
   c) They should be kept by senior managers ❑
   d) They should be locked up ❑

3. Should managers (in the view of the writer and many others) be held responsible for costs that are not within their control?
   a) Always ❑
   b) Usually ❑
   c) Not usually ❑
   d) Of course not ❑

4. Which of the following is a feature of absorption costing?
   a) All costs are allocated to individual products or cost centres ❑
   b) It is very interesting (or sometimes even absorbing) ❑
   c) Fixed costs are disregarded ❑
   d) Variable costs are disregarded ❑

5. Which of the following can be entirely allocated to individual products?
   a) Indirect wages ❑
   b) Rent ❑
   c) Direct wages ❑
   d) The salary of the managing director ❑

6. Which of the following is not a valid way of allocating non-direct costs?
   a) According to the wishes of the government ❑
   b) Pro-rata to production hours ❑
   c) Pro-rata to machine hours ❑
   d) Pro-rata to direct labour costs ❑

7. A business sells watches for £10 each. Fixed costs are £10,000 and indirect costs are £5 per watch. Referring to a break-even chart, if you can prepare one, how many watches must be sold before break-even point is reached?
   a) 1,500 ❑
   b) 2,000 ❑
   c) 2,500 ❑
   d) 3,000 ❑

8. Using the information in question 7 above, how many watches must be sold to achieve break-even if the costs are unchanged but the selling price is reduced to £8?

a) 2,500 ☐
b) 3,000 ☐
c) 3,334 ☐
d) 3,667 ☐

9. Which of the following would be true in the event of the variable cost being greater than the selling price?

a) The more units sold the more the loss would increase ☐
b) Variable costs would have to be reallocated ☐
c) The more units sold the more the loss would reduce ☐
d) The directors would have to resign (just joking) ☐

10. Standard material cost per unit of production £5
Actual production 3,000 units
Actual material cost £15,500
What is the material usage variance?

a) £1,000 unfavourable ☐
b) £500 unfavourable ☐
c) £500 favourable ☐
d) £1,000 favourable ☐

SUNDAY

MONDAY

TUESDAY

WEDNESDAY

THURSDAY

FRIDAY

SATURDAY

SATURDAY

Budgets

Budgeting is probably the element of finance that has most impact on the time of non-financial managers and for this reason most of them have at least some knowledge of the subject. Of course, some non-financial managers resent this time commitment and see budgeting as an unproductive chore. It can be, but this should not be the case if it is handled well and budget relationships are understood.

We will look at:

- budgeting in different types of organization
- the profit budget
- the sales budget
- revenue expenditure budgets
- the capital expenditure budget
- cash and the Balance Sheet
- after the budget has been approved.

Budgeting in different types of organization

In very large organizations, hundreds of managers may be involved in the budgeting process, and the complete budget will probably be a very thick document. This would be true of, say, a National Health Service Trust and in the private sector of companies such as Shell.

This involvement takes a lot of management time but, if the budgeting is done well, it is likely to be time well spent. This is because the budget will probably be a realistic one, and because after approval the managers should feel committed to it.

When the budget has been approved, individual managers are responsible for their section of it. The responsibility is like a pyramid. At the base of the pyramid are the most junior managers, supervising a comparatively small section, perhaps involving expenditure only. These junior managers should, however, have some knowledge of the overall budget and objectives.

In the middle may be more senior managers and divisional directors, each with a wider area of responsibility for achieving the complete budget objectives. If everyone else meets their targets they will have an easy job.

Budgets should be designed to meet the needs of a particular organization and its managers. For example, a large school could well have an expenditure budget of about £4,000,000. There will be little income and the budgeting emphasis will be on capital expenditure and revenue expenditure. The main aims will be informed choice and value for money.

The rest of today's work is devoted to the budget of a large company because this best illustrates the main principles. However, a smaller organization should budget using the same methods. There will be fewer managers involved, and less paper, but the same procedures should be followed.

On Sunday, we considered Julia Brown's book, and on Monday we considered John Brown's gardening business. Even their budgets follow the same principles. John Brown's van and motor mower constitute his capital expenditure budget. In their case the budgets will probably be on just one or two pieces of paper.

The profit budget

There are usually several budgets and they all impact on each other. The profit budget is arguably the most important and this is considered first.

There are two basic approaches to budgeting in a large organization, both having advantages and disadvantages.

- The so-called 'bottom up' method. Proposals are taken from the lower management levels. These are collated into an overall budget that may or may not be acceptable. If it is not, then top management calls for revisions.
- The so-called 'top down' method. Top management issues budget targets. Lower levels of management must then submit proposals that achieve these targets.

In practice, there is often less difference between the two methods than might be supposed. It is important that at some stage there is a full and frank exchange of views. Everyone should be encouraged to put forward any constructive point of view, and everyone should commit themselves to listening with an open mind. Needless to say, top management will, and should, have the final decisions.

It is a common mistake for managers to be too insular and to overlook what changes competitors are making.

All the budgets are important but in a commercial organization the overall profit budget is likely to be considered the most important. A summarized six-month profit budget for a large organization is given below.

Kingston Staplers Ltd – Profit Budget for half year

	January	February	March	April	May	June	Total half year
	£000	£000	£000	£000	£000	£000	£000
Sales							
UK	1,500	1,400	1,450	1,700	1,600	1,800	9,450
Export	200	220	180	190	400	340	1,530
	1,700	1,620	1,630	1,890	2,000	2,140	10,980
Less cost of sales	1,020	970	990	1,150	1,230	1,320	6,680
Gross Profit	680	650	640	740	770	820	4,300
Overheads							
Sales Department	200	220	230	210	210	220	1,290
Finance Department	190	200	180	190	220	210	1,190
Administration Department	230	240	250	250	250	260	1,480
Total overheads	620	660	660	650	680	690	3,960
Net Profit/(Loss)	60	(10)	(20)	90	90	130	340

Please particularly note the following points:

- Most budgets are for a year but this is not a requirement. They can be for six months or for any other useful period.
- This budget gives monthly figures, which is the most common division, but again this is not fixed. The divisions can be weekly, quarterly, or some other period.
- The figures are summarized in thousands of pounds.
- This is suitable for a summary budget of a large organization. The budgets leading up to these summarized figures will be more detailed. January's budget for postage might, for example, be £2,850.
- As we will see, various subsidiary budgets and calculations feed figures through to this summary budget.

The sales budget

This should be in sufficient detail for management to know the sources of revenue. The figures will be broken down into different products and different sales regions. Each regional sales manager will have responsibility for a part of the sales budget. A section of the sales budget might look like the following:

Scottish Region Sales Budget

	Jan £	Feb £	March £
Product A	16,000	12,000	17,000
Product B	13,000	13,000	13,000
Product C	40,000	45,000	50,000
	69,000	70,000	80,000

Before the sales budget is done it would be normal for top management to issue budget assumptions concerning prices, competition, and other key matters.

The sales budget will be for orders taken. There will usually be a timing difference before orders become invoiced sales.

Revenue expenditure budgets

Still using the example of Kingston Staplers Ltd, the cost of sales will consist of direct wages, items bought for resale, raw materials and so on. The Sales, Finance, and Administration Departments will make up the overhead budget. In practice, this overhead budget is likely to be divided into three, with a different manager responsible for each section.

As with all the other budgets, each manager should submit a detailed budget for the section for which he or she is responsible.

As with the sales budget, top management should give initial guidance on expected performance and policy assumptions. For example, a manager might be told to assume a company-wide average pay rise of 5% on 1 April.

The capital expenditure budget

This is extremely significant in some companies, less so in others. It will list all the planned capital expenditure showing the date when the expenditure will be made, and the date that the expenditure will be completed and the asset introduced to the business. Major contracts may be payable in instalments and the timing is important to the cash budget.

A sum for miscellaneous items is usually necessary. For example, major projects might be listed separately and then £15,000 per month added for all projects individually less than £5,000.

Within the capital expenditure budget, timing is very important. Expenditure affects cash and interest straight away. Depreciation usually starts only on completion.

Cash and the Balance Sheet

When the profit budgets are complete, it is important that a cash budget is prepared. This is a Cash-Flow Forecast, which was examined in detail on Thursday. You might like to spend a few minutes referring back to this.

In practice, the profit budget and cash budget are linked and a chicken and egg problem has to be resolved. The profit budget cannot be completed until the interest figure is available. This in turn depends on the cash budget. The cash budget depends partly on the profit budget.

Dilemmas like this are quite common in budgeting. It is usual to put in an estimated figure for interest and then adjust everything later if necessary. This can be very time-consuming, and budgeting is much simpler if it is computerized. Several hours' work can be reduced to minutes and management is much freer to test budgets with useful 'what if' questions.

You will recall that one of Monday's accounting rules stated that every debit has a credit. It follows that every figure in the budgets has a forecastable consequence in a future Balance

Sheet. It is normal to conclude the budgets by preparing a month-by-month forecast Balance Sheet and bankers are likely to ask for this. It may be that some aspect of the Balance Sheet is unacceptable and a partial re-budget is necessary.

In practice, top management is likely to review and alter some aspects of the budgets several times.

After the budget has been approved

After the budget has been approved comes . . . quite possibly nothing at all. This is a pity but it does not mean that the budgeting exercise has been a complete waste of time. The participants will have thought logically about the organization, its finances and its future. Some of the detail will remain in their minds and influence their future actions.

Nevertheless, the budgets will be much more valuable if they are used in an active way. Regular performance reports should be issued by the accountants. These should be in the same format as the budgets, and should give comparable budget and actual figures. Variances should also be given.

All levels of management should regularly review these figures and explain the variances. Significant variances will pose the question of whether corrective action needs to be taken.

Finally, budgets do not necessarily have to be done just once a year. They may be updated, reviewed, or even scrapped and redone as circumstances dictate.

Summary

Finance affects the jobs of virtually all non-financial managers and during this week you should have significantly increased your knowledge of the subject. Many elements of finance have been examined and much ground has been covered.

The following summarizes the subjects studied:

Profit Statements (Sunday)

A simple example

A trading company and a manufacturing company

Further concepts

A full example

Balance Sheets (Monday)

What is a Balance Sheet?

Accounting rules and a simple example

Further concepts

Test your knowledge

Published accounts (Tuesday)

Availability of published accounts

Profit and Loss Account and Balance Sheet

SUNDAY
MONDAY
TUESDAY
WEDNESDAY
THURSDAY
FRIDAY
SATURDAY

Other items included in published accounts

Accounting ratios and investment decisions (Wednesday)
Accounting ratios explained
Understanding accounting ratios
Investment decisions

Cash and the management of working capital (Thursday)
Distinctions between cash and profit
The Cash-Flow Forecast
The management of working capital

Costing (Friday)
The value and uses of costing
Absorption costing
Break-even charts
Marginal costing and standard costing

Budgets (Saturday)
The profit budget and associated budgets
The capital expenditure budget
Cash and the Balance Sheet
After the budget has been approved

Fact-check (answers at the back)

1. In a very large company individual junior managers each have responsibility for a relatively small cost centre. Which phrase best describes their cost centres' place in the overall company budget?
   - a) In the centre of the circle ❏
   - b) At the edge of the rectangle ❏
   - c) At the base of the pyramid ❏
   - d) Pulsating in the pentagon ❏

2. A large company has a full set of budgets. Which of the following statements should be true?
   - a) They should all be independent of each other ❏
   - b) Some should impact on each other ❏
   - c) The capital expenditure budget should not affect the other budgets ❏
   - d) They should all impact on each other ❏

3. Which of the following is a feature of the so-called 'top down' method of budgeting?
   - a) Top management issues budget targets ❏
   - b) Lower management issues budget proposals without prior guidance ❏
   - c) There are frequent meetings
   - d) Only revenue budgets are required ❏

4. Must budgets cover a period of a year?
   - a) No – and they usually cover a period of six months ❏
   - b) No – but they often do ❏
   - c) No – and they never do ❏
   - d) Yes ❏

5. In a big company in what way is it normal for the sales budget to be broken down?
   - a) By region ❏
   - b) By period ❏
   - c) By product ❏
   - d) By all of the above ❏

6. When does capital expenditure usually start to affect cash and interest?
   - a) When the orders are placed ❏
   - b) When the capital items are brought into use ❏
   - c) When payment is made ❏
   - d) When depreciation starts ❏

7. How important is the cash budget likely to be?
   - a) Important ❏
   - b) Not very important ❏
   - c) Not at all important ❏
   - d) A complete waste of time ❏

8. Can the capital expenditure budget be altered without the balance sheet budget being affected?
   - a) Yes ❏
   - b) Sometimes ❏
   - c) Not usually ❏
   - d) No ❏

9. What should happen after the budgets have been approved?
a) Nothing ☐
b) It should be kept available for inspection when required ☐
c) Top managers should look at them from time to time ☐
d) All levels of management should regularly review actual and budget figures and explain the variances ☐

10. What are the advantages in involving all levels of management in budget preparation?
a) The budget is more likely to be realistic ☐
b) Managers are more likely to feel committed to it ☐
c) It may be good for morale ☐
d) All of the above ☐

Surviving in tough times

A basic understanding of finance is always important but never more so than when times are tough. At the very least, profits may be down or losses may be made. There will probably be cutbacks and every penny will count. Pay may be frozen and jobs may be lost. Even worse, businesses may have to close.

Mastering the basics of finance will help you understand the problems and take steps to minimize the damage. It should assist you personally, and it should help you manage the downturn and lay the foundations for future prosperity. Here are ten crucial tips to help you do it.

1 Never forget the importance of cash

Remember the saying 'Cash is King'. Losses may eventually force a business to close but in the short term, lack of cash is likely to be the critical factor. You should hoard cash and you should plan your cash flow very carefully – daily if necessary. Talk to your bank early and explain your plans. Cash should be the number one priority.

2 Never forget the importance of working capital

Working capital is the difference between assets realizable in the short term and liabilities payable in the short term. It includes cash held and money owed. Quickly realizable assets are the next best thing to cash. If you can get the working capital right, you should be safe. Try hard to achieve this.

3 Get your customers to pay on time

Take it seriously and give the task the time and resources necessary. Tell yourself that you are entitled to be paid on time and that you are being cheated if you are not. Agree the terms in advance and make it clear that they should be honoured. A good motto is 'ask early and ask often'. If all else fails take legal action. A tough but fair line will probably not upset your customers, but it might. Ask yourself if you really want those customers.

4 Try to get a long-term loan

A bank overdraft is repayable on demand. A long-term loan is repayable at a future date, or more likely in instalments over a period. If times are hard (or even if they are not), there are obvious advantages to having a long-term loan instead of an overdraft, or as well as an overdraft. So long as you do not breach the terms of the agreement, you cannot be forced to pay it back quickly. This gives you peace of mind.

5 Keep an eye on the accounting ratios

These were explained on Wednesday. They are always useful, but are particularly so if a business is in trouble. You should know what is acceptable and you should monitor trends over a period. If things are going wrong, this may spotlight the dangers and indicate where remedial action is needed. Gearing and the number of days' credit given and taken may be especially useful.

6 Use the financial figures quickly

Financial data should help you survive tough times and it will be more valuable if you can get it quickly and use it quickly. It is sometimes better to have slightly inaccurate or incomplete information quickly than perfect information some time later. Talk this over with your financial colleagues. Make time to look at it and act on it when it comes.

7 Be sceptical about expert advice

Experts will probably give you good advice, but do not overlook the possibility that they may be mistaken. For centuries, experts said that the world was flat, but Christopher Columbus proved them wrong. Experts (who were paid a lot of money) or some of them at least, failed to foresee and plan for the economic mess that has plagued much of the world. You may not be a financial expert but you are probably an expert at your particular job. If the advice feels wrong, perhaps it *is* wrong.

8 Do not drown in financial detail

You may be given a vast amount of financial information, particularly if you work for a large company. This could be because someone believes that it is useful or just because the system automatically provides it. Remember the old saying about not being able to see the wood for trees. Learn to concentrate on what is important and give little or no attention to the rest. That way you will get the key financial information and still have time to do your job. This is particularly important when things are tough and your time is at a premium.

9 Do not overlook the value of marginal costing

When times are tough there is likely to be pressure on sales and margins. In this situation, marginal costing – which was explained on Friday – could be very helpful. It may be essential to cut fixed costs and it may be necessary to adjust prices. Marginal costing should help you make the right decisions.

10 Prevention is better than cure

There is an old joke about a man being asked the way to Trafalgar Square. He is supposed to have replied: 'If I was going to Trafalgar Square I would not be starting from here'. It is good to be able to get out of financial difficulties but it is better not to have financial difficulties in the first place. The intelligent and timely use of financial information can help avoid them. It is tempting not to plan and budget in the good times, but it is probably a mistake.

Answers

Sunday: 1b; 2a; 3d; 4a; 5b; 6c; 7b; 8d; 9c; 10a.

Monday: 1c; 2b; 3d; 4a; 5c; 6a; 7c; 8b; 9d; 10a.

Tuesday: 1c; 2d; 3a; 4a; 5c; 6b; 7b; 8a; 9d; 10a.

Wednesday: 1c; 2c; 3b; 4c; 5d; 6b; 7a; 8b; 9b; 10d.

Thursday: 1a; 2b; 3d; 4c; 5d; 6c; 7d; 8a and d; 9a and c; 10c.

Friday: 1b; 2b; 3d; 4a; 5c; 6a; 7b; 8c; 9a; 10b.

Saturday: 1c; 2d; 3a; 4b; 5d; 6c; 7a; 8d; 9d; 10d.

Glossary

Absorption Costing A costing system that involves all indirect costs being allocated to individual products or cost centres.

Accruals Costs for which value has been received, but which have not yet been entered into the books of account.

Bad Debt A debt that cannot be recovered and has to be written off.

Break-Even Point The level of sales at which revenue equals the sum of fixed costs plus variable costs.

Capital Expenditure Expenditure on items of a capital nature, i.e. assets that will have a long-term value.

Consolidated Accounts The accounts of a holding company incorporating the accounts of all its subsidiary companies.

Contingencies Costs that may be incurred in the future, e.g. the cost of settling a pending legal action.

Cost Of Sales The cost of items sold (includes purchase price and manufacturing cost, but excludes overheads).

Creditor Person or business to whom money is owed.

Current Assets Assets with a value available in the short term (usually taken to be less than a year).

Current Liabilities Liabilities which may have to be paid off in the short term (usually taken to be less than a year).

Debtor Person or business that owes money to you.

Depreciation The proportion of the cost of a fixed asset charged to the Profit and Loss account in a given period.

Dividend Per Share The total dividends for the year divided by the number of shares in issue.

Fixed Assets Assets that have a long-term value and will generate revenue in the long term.

Fixed Costs Costs that do not vary according to the volume of activity, e.g. business rates.

Gearing The ratio between finance provided by the banks and other borrowing and the finance invested by the shareholders.

Gross Profit Profit after deducting direct costs of manufacture and purchase, but without deducting overheads.

Net Profit Profit after deducting all costs including overheads. It is sometimes expressed as 'Net Profit Before Tax' and sometimes as 'Net Profit After Tax'.

Payback The period of time in which savings caused by capital expenditure equal the amount of the capital expenditure. No account is taken of interest.

Prepayments Costs entered into the books of account for which the value has not yet been received.

Price/Earnings Ratio The current price per share divided by earnings per share.

Standard Costs Pre-set standard costs from which actual costs are measured.

Stock Shrinkage Reduction in stock caused by theft, evaporation, or similar causes.

Stock Turn The number of times that total stock is used (turned over) in the course of a year.

Variable Costs Costs that vary according to the volume of activity, e.g. direct wages.

Working Capital The amount by which current assets exceed current liabilities.

ALSO AVAILABLE IN THE 'IN A WEEK' SERIES

SUCCESSFUL JOB APPLICATIONS • SUCCESSFUL JOB HUNTING
• SUCCESSFUL KEY ACCOUNT MANAGEMENT • SUCCESSFUL LEADERSHIP
• SUCCESSFUL MARKETING • SUCCESSFUL MARKETING PLANS
• SUCCESSFUL MEETINGS • SUCCESSFUL MEMORY TECHNIQUES
• SUCCESSFUL MENTORING • SUCCESSFUL NEGOTIATING • SUCCESSFUL
NETWORKING • SUCCESSFUL PEOPLE SKILLS • SUCCESSFUL
PRESENTING • SUCCESSFUL PROJECT MANAGEMENT • SUCCESSFUL
PSYCHOMETRIC TESTING • SUCCESSFUL PUBLIC RELATIONS •
SUCCESSFUL RECRUITMENT • SUCCESSFUL SELLING • SUCCESSFUL
STRATEGY • SUCCESSFUL TIME MANAGEMENT • TACKLING INTERVIEW
QUESTIONS

For information about other titles in the series, please visit www.inaweek.co.uk

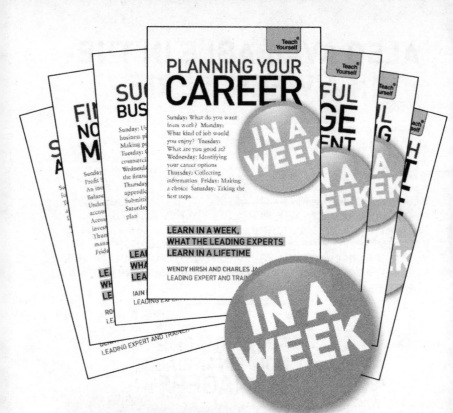